SHARPSBURG

SHARPSBURG
A CIVIL WAR NARRATIVE

BY KENT GRAMM

RESOURCE *Publications* · Eugene, Oregon

SHARPSBURG
A Civil War Narrative

Reource Publications
An Imprint of Wipf and Stock Publishers
199 W. 8th Ave., Suite 3
Eugene, OR 97401

www.wipfandstock.com

ISBN 13: 978-1-4982-3906-6

Manufactured in the U.S.A.   11/23/2015

For
YVONNE FRINK
and
CHRIS HEISEY

If we could understand its loves,
as well as its hates, we would be nearer
understanding the mystery of human life.

—John Keegan on the First World War

To the Reader

In the summer of 2015, the Confederate battle flag came down from the South Carolina state capitol; but in the late summer of 1862 it flew higher than it ever had or ever would again. A summer of brilliant campaigns and costly victories had brought the army of Robert E. Lee and Stonewall Jackson across the Potomac in an invasion of the North. President Abraham Lincoln promised his God that if slow-moving General McClellan and his Army of the Potomac won a victory, he would issue a proclamation freeing all slaves in the rebellious states. Thus the bloodiest day in American history, the Battle of Antietam, called Sharpsburg by Southerners, became the battle where the war for the Union became a war against slavery.

This is a story of that battle, told by two participants. One fought for the South, the other for the Union. Their ghostly voices still speak for rebellion and equality, and still haunt the American arguments about freedom and race.

Army of Northern Virginia, Confederate States

I am a Rebel

Now, everyone is born a rebel or
a unionist. I wonder which you are.
Might could be, you aren't what you think you are.

I was a Rebel and I'm still a Rebel.
I'm not ashamed to tell you what I was
and what I am. Some say the War is over
but I have yet to see the evidence.
We are still here. Sharpsburg is anything
but in the past. September Seventeenth
of Sixty-Two: the worst day of the War.
The thing went on another thirty months
and several times we could have won it back,
but the Confederacy was killed that day
along Antietam Creek in Maryland;
it's just we didn't know it for awhile.
That was one day—a day to wish undone,
if but the Good Lord worked that way. That day
the War became a war to free the slaves—
became so by old Abe Lincoln's order.

Of course our institution was the war,
but be that as it may, I'm here to tell
you true: I didn't enlist for slavery,
except I wasn't about to permit
some damnyankee government, tell me what
exactly I might do and how and when.
If you were born with rights and property,
you wouldn't give them up without a fight.
I did not join this fight for slavery
personally, but for the principle.
My household owned no servant property,
but would defend to the death a man's right
to ownership, however rich or poor.
A lot of good it did us in the end.
I rue it all some days; on better days
I'd do it all again. A man must learn
there comes a time in every decent life
to fight Yankees, whatever form they come.
Possession might be nine-tenths of the law,
but Rights are all the law and what it's for.
That is the truth. That is the Rebel truth.
So I will tell the truth and nothing but
the truth and many other things
to supplement the truth, so help me God.

Freedom

Freedom is the let-alone all of us
Americans receive when we are born,
a trust passed down from every Patriot
who left his home and family to die

in battle for the cause of Liberty.
Our word for this was Rights. For Rights we pledged
our lives, our liberties, and sacred honor
to the South. At bottom, we'd not be told,
right or wrong, what to do; and they
would just as soon kill every one of us
as let us go our way. Their righteousness
was such that they'd invent a new machine
to kill us with for every point of conscience
in their busy minds, for our property
offended them, was our liability.
They shouldered our responsibilities
because to them freedom was for someone
else, always someone else, whether children,
servants of their betters, posterity,
or anyone in need of fixing as they
saw fit. A man can't live with such people.
It's worse than having a churchgoing wife
who's always better than you, and tells you.

Across the Potomac

The Old Man knew what he was doing. General
Robert E. Lee: the name still sets the heart
afire, and I would follow him again,
right or wrong, as I did in September
1862, the summer of our lives.
The Old Man ordered us across the river
because it was the only move he had.
The victories in Virginia had run
their course, and we could wait

to be destroyed—which happened, sure enough,
two summers and a winter later—or
we could turn the Federal army out
of its forts and dirt around Washington
and break them up this one last time for good.
We had sufficient men; don't be deceived
by our reports of what befell us later:
a Southerner is hardly better than
a damnyankee if he cannot exaggerate
with honor, and face outrages, insults,
and near universal odds like a man.
The General was no fool: he took a good
fifty, sixty thousand up, the best men
we ever had—a lean and hungry set
of wolves, one woman said who watched us cross
the River, tough and confident and strong
from chasing Yankees, two whole armies of them,
all the summer long, and just last week killed
them worst of all at Manassas. Our guns
were clean and polished, though our shoes were thin
or gone; no two of us were dressed alike;
we talked incessantly, profane beyond
belief, that same woman reported of us—
though how she stood it close enough to tell
escapes me, because of course we smelled like hell.
A doctor up in Fredericktown would count us
next week, accurate to the point of throwing
in the scientific observation that
our smell was "amoniacal." It was,
if you weren't used to it. I wish it had
been strong enough to mask the smell of blood

on battlefields—the metal sweet, lead-kneed
odor all the rivers in the world can't
wash out of your stomach. We splashed across
the River at the ford, some men bundling
their amoniacal long johns atop
their heads—I trust that woman's modesty
and decency prevented her from watching
close up, although who'd give a damn: a line
of hairy scarecrows in their shirts. We crossed
the River. Bands, our execrable bands,
played "Maryland, My Maryland," and we
like young fools sang along and whooped it up.
It was the summer of the Confederacy
and the shipwreck of our hopes was around
the bend invisible. The sun shone South.
We were invincible, and we could whip
the Yankees ten to one, although to tell
the truth we had died more numerously
than they had all the summer, but that fact
was like an untruth to a Southerner:
an insult not to be tolerated
where rights and honor are at stake. In fact
some thousands politely declined to cross
because it seemed not right to them to strike
the unionists on their home ground as they
were striking us. The Golden Rule or prudence,
don't know which and didn't care. We crossed fast
within the grasp of victories whose logic
ordered us to wade the swirling waters
of necessity. Our black folk followed,
driving miles and miles of wagons filled

with fodder, bandages, and ammunition.

The men who carried doubts across the river
or declined to cross because they wouldn't do
to others what they'd done to us were few
compared to us of less fastidious thought
who'd had enough of Yankee righteousness.
We'd take the war to them—we'd take the war
to hell and back—to finish it this month.
We'd whipped them running all the summer long
and had the notion we could do anything.
We hated them enough to die in droves,
and you would too, if you were us, in love
with freedom to do what we pleased and told
that we were sinful by inferiors,
by Yankees—money-grubbers culled
from prisons, slums, and what-not, Europe's
dregs, ill-mannered, unrefined, and reeking
of the greasy coal their factories spewed.
We Southerners were disinclined to serve
a government—paid for by Southerners,
mind you—a government that had gone foul,
was lording over us majorities
of rough-scruff rubbish from the alleys
of New York. Like our fathers and grandfathers,
we would be our own men or die proving
it. And we had. We had outfought the Yankees
through the summer and knew it, knew we had
to beat them now and finish it before
we were bled out. You may say we were daring
and you might say we were arrogant, but

it was desperation and necessity
that led and pushed us into the Potomac,
run like foxes by the hounds of our own
success. We yelled and cheered as we went down
to the River, wild with defiance, shoeless
lords with snapping flags, free men with no choice
but to lay those flags before the Lord of Lords,
the God of Battles.
              Some say sixty thousand
crossed—that doctor counted more—as many,
nearly, as the Federals—but we frittered
down to forty-five, they say, by the time
we got to Sharpsburg, though the Yankees wouldn't
know it. Then how we came to lose so many
of our men I now commence to tell you.
The Yankees had a thing or two to do
with our eventual disappointment,
and chief among them was their president,
a man we scorned and ridiculed. We said,
"Jeff Davis rode a dapple gray; Abe Lincoln
rode a mule." But that was a tough old mule.
All Yankeedom went shrieking like a flock
of geese when word of us raced North. Invasion!
Rebel Army Marching on Washington!
Except that man in the White House. He stood
looking out his window west and thinking,
"Come on, come on closer," like some canny
farmer luring in a fox close enough
not to miss this time, tying down a pullet
by one scrawny ankle so it will flap
and squawk like crazy while the fox drifts closer,

pacing in the brush, calculating, hungry;
and the farmer slowly raises his trusty
old musket to his shoulder—the same one
his daddy used in 1812—and bang!
We didn't know who we were challenging,
or what, and so we swung route-step into
two long arms, stronger than Lincoln's. Our God
was simpler than Lincoln's, understandable,
more down-home and reassuring, righteous
in a predictable way. Who or what
Abe prayed to I don't know, but he promised
his tall God, some steady-eyed Mystery,
that if the Union boys could lick us this
one time, the president would strike us hard
through our black folk. That God was somewhere
on the battlefield, you might say. Some say
there is no God on battlefields but Chance.
It's beyond me. But some necessity,
carried by that President like a plague,
cornered us at Sharpsburg. Old Abe Lincoln
didn't scare. Say what you will about Little
Mac, he thought he was outnumbered and still
came after us. Slow as sap at first, but
sure.
        The Old Man split us up like rebels,
sent us out all over Maryland, hither
and yon, to snatch supplies and generally
raise hell—"confuse and mystify," Old Jack
used to say. And speaking of Old Jack, Marse
Robert sent him down with half the army

own's

gan,

e must have

and

ling,

s—until

eless

like fire in a dry cornfield. D. H. Hill's
division saw their campfires from all along
South Mountain, and never felt so alone,
with the scattered pieces of our army
miles to the west, and Jackson down across
the river—eighty or ninety thousand
Yankees coming, and hell following after.

own view of Northerners.

60 000 → 45 000

1812 → ??

McClellan.

Army of the Potomac, United States

The Army of the Free

The free are not free, only think they are—
but that makes all the difference in the world.
A soldier does exactly what he's told,
more or less—such is life, and such is war:
nothing comes without its opposite.
To save your freedoms you become not free:
you fight for peace, and kill your enemies.
To save his life, the poet sits and writes,
renouncing everything for poetry.
And they went in and died to save their rights.

The poet calls on God to help him out—
I do so here—surrendering his mind,
though not his heart, and giving all to doubt.
The soldier writes his fortunes on the wind
and marches down a road of circumstance,
his every step a metrical decline
from that unchosen, free Nothing whence
he came. He is a child of God and chance
begotten in a short, shocking romance.

He lives only to hold that shaky line.

*

We saw the President in Washington
a few days after we had lost Bull Run
again—Old Abe the railsplitter, shirt-sleeved,
tilting awkward-tall as a whooping crane
over four soldiers on the White House lawn.
His lined face showed both cheerfulness and grief.
Wounded boys lay everywhere. He had come
out carrying a pail of lemonade
and got to talking. He was a good man.
You wanted to say, "We'll do all we can,

Old Abe. We'll settle up with them at the next
dance." We knew the Rebs had crossed the Potomac
and filled the roads of central Maryland.
But it would be all right. Our Little Mac
would stir the Army back in shape and deal
with Bobby Lee at the right time. *Our man,*
McClellan was, like none after. To feel
devoted to a general makes an army—
the saucy graybacks had it; so did we.
You needed more than uniforms and steel

to win battles, and Mister Lincoln's army,
the Army of the Potomac, would stay
the course until the gentlemen in gray,
who put their rights and so-called "property"

ahead of Old Glory and posterity,
would yield to justice and to law. Today
the Army rests, tomorrow binds its wounds,
and on the third day rises, shouldering
its knapsacks and its muskets to the sound
of its own bugles, and our men will sing

"John Brown's Body" and "Rally Round the Flag,"
and we will meet them now on our own dear
Northern soil. We stepped with little straggling
in our brigade this time, and somewhere near
Frederick the pace picked up as if some charge
of lightning had been fed to headquarters.
You could sense sterner purpose in the march.
Some Indiana boys had found Lee's orders
and now Little Mac and our generals knew
the Rebs had split. Now we knew what to do.

South Mountain

On the fourteenth we marched to South Mountain
from our camp near Frederick. The day was warm
and many of the boys just shed their twenty
extra cartridges. Carry sixty pounds
of knapsack, rations, steel—and there's more harm
in too much weight than waste. Forty's plenty.
Your piece would foul before you'd get past forty.
The Rebels bragged about how light they marched,
and so they did. And how, their blacks could tell.
We hoisted ours and carried it ourselves.

The Black Hat brigade drew the hardest task—
up Turner's Gap astride the National Road.
It's nothing but a steep ravine: trees, rocks,
and Rebels with that hatred in their souls
for Yanks that only Southerners can nurse—
two lines of them looking down at you behind
their muskets' sights, smiling. A fifty-eight
calibre ball would knock you on your arse,
shatter bones, remove your face, or if fate
were kind, kill you. Such is the force of hate.

Our Little Mac was watching two miles back.
At first our rifles shone golden—the sun
a mass of yellow fire as we attacked
their skirmishers on green and level ground;
then silver, as we ascended the shadowed
slope in sudden twilight—our lines did slow
but did not stop; now bronze, lit by discharges
veiled in drifting gray: marching to Zion,
marching to Zion, something drove us hard.
McClellan said, "They must be made of iron."

So we were named the Iron Brigade. That night
we stayed on the slope of South Mountain, not
quite at the top but close enough, not licked
and not going back down, slept with our heads
behind stones and trees and those who were shot.

In the morning the graybacks had gone, quick
as rabbits in the night. The way was open.
The Army of the Potomac poured through. One division
removed their caps, saluting us. We took it in our stride,
and left our friends dead on the mountainside.

Army of Northern Virginia

Orders in the Hands of God

The Book of Revelation has a scroll
of writing coming out an angel's mouth
as if to say, "These words are from the Lord."
Well, Lee's orders made in duplicate sent
to all four corners of our army found
their men. Stonewall Jackson committed them
to memory, then tore the order up;
and so did Lafayette McLaws, promptly.
Old Peter Longstreet, making sure, reversed
the picture in Revelation, stuffing
the paper into his mouth—chewed it up
and spat the ugly mush back out—as good
as never issued, except in his mind.
And Harvey Hill was many things, but careless
was not one of them. Yet he was blamed.
As good a general as he was, he never
could get right with the Old Man, or Jackson,
or anybody else. His own men liked
him well enough. He thought well and fought well
but seemed meant to be alone, which is how
he spent most of the war after Sharpsburg:

independent command, outposts, defenses—
brooding on the Will of God perhaps: why,
exactly, someone dropped a copy, wrapped
around three seegars; and why, exactly,
some damnyankee soldier boys happened to
take a rest in just that field, in that green
pasture, beside some still water, and spot
those seegars with the sharp eye only Yanks
have got, and bored or thinking, actually read
the paper tied with string around the smokes—
signed by Lee's adjutant, the signature
recognized by a Yankee officer—
and that, they say, made all the difference.
Well, I don't know. You'd like to think nobody
beat us, short of God Himself, least of all
an army full of nothing but Yankees—
but that Potomac army was the best
of any on the planet, except for one
which modesty forbids my mentioning.
Which is why I say Never, do not ever,
underestimate a people who fight
for principle, however self-righteous,
irreligious, and murderous it is.
I am saying that the reason the Army
of the Potomac had the dumb luck
or was given our plans by the clean hand
of Providence, was that they were coming
after us in the first place. Those Yankee
boys in that meadow were on our track, if
the truth be told. They had been whipped all summer,
outgeneralled and humiliated,

but they were not defeated. We were better,
keep in mind, so let them come: we would turn
and fight them. And that is what Harvey Hill
did, his men all alone, the way he wanted,
on South Mountain, while the rest of the Army
tried to concentrate. See, many a time
our fast-marching boys would be forced to tell
a gaggle of chatty Marylanders,
"Beg pardon, we are a-tryin' to think."
Well then, sometimes I've wondered what a battle
is a concentration of—rage, hatred,
fear, nobility, the devil's spite; or
the deep and awful, gracious will of God—
or underneath it nothing like those things
at all, just chance. But what were the chances
in that farmer's field, that our enemies
would find our orders so they could know what
to do? What concentration of the sky
appeared in that small field? Are blades of grass
planted by God's hand? Are God's marching orders
issued everywhere, copies stored in stones,
instructions in the beauty of the lilies—
His strategies strung somehow in the fragile
maps of the spider's web, his plans waiting
as plain as the day, visible to us
and invisible to us? These quiet
fields are filled with unheard thunder, called up
by a voice we don't hear. They have been spun
of the same stuff as angel wings; so we
spot only now and then, in fields murmuring
with careless voices, orders He has written.

*

We Stand and Fight

As in your sleep you tell your legs to run
but they don't move; they are slow and heavy
like in water, chest pressing against water—
that was the nightmare of the long, late night
of the fourteenth, and the seared-eyed, parched-mouthed
stumbling morning of the fifteenth. Hill's men,
staggering from all day's fighting back at
South Mountain, mortified beyond all speech
to be running from the hordes of Yankees
for the first time, and damned if not the last,
skedaddling from the damnyankee army—
and damned thankful to get out with their lives—
ordered by the Old Man toward the River:
take the roads to Sharpsburg, cross the River
there, get back into Virginia before
the Federal army crushes every piece
of our five-way scattered band of brothers.
Longstreet's boys marched fast from north and west while
McLaws, about to be caught by Yankees
to his north while he faced south at Harper's
Ferry, training his guns at the Federal
arsenal and garrison, wondered what
to do: escape himself, or obey orders
calling for his men to block escape from
Harper's Ferry by the Yanks? Walker's men
stood on the heights across the River, east
of Harper's Ferry, and Stonewall Jackson—
childish, I admit, the names we make up

in war, but in this case a solid comfort—
Stonewall with the largest part of the corps
circled Harper's south and west, demanding
surrender. The Yankees helped us out—we
thought. Green troops ran back into town, letting
us have the heights on all sides, and when we
opened with artillery all around,
well, the officer in charge of those twelve
thousand men thought, It's only a question
of time; might as well surrender now—save
some lives anyhow. If he'd have held on
one more day, there would have been no fight
at Sharpsburg. But he didn't hold on. So
Deacon Jackson in his usual way, giving
praise to God but in the end not knowing
for what, sent General Lee a little note:
"Through God's blessing," he wrote, Harper's Ferry,
with its stock of cannons, small arms, wagons,
food, and Yankees was to be offered up—
surrendered presently, that is; and that
did it.

      Now, when the surrender took place,
the Yankee boys all stretched to get a look
at Mighty Stonewall. They were disappointed.
"He isn't much for looks," one said, "but if
we'd had him, boys, we wouldn't have been caught
in this trap." A reporter from New York—
New York Times no less, a man of taste—wrote
that Stonewall cut a shabby figure, dressed
in coarse homespun, worn and grimy; a hat
the likes of which any Northern beggar

would refuse if offered—in short a seedy
tramp no different in appearance from those
bearded, barefoot tramps that followed him—which
would have made you wonder, wouldn't it, whether
God weren't on the Southern side after all?
"They glory in their shame," the reporter
wrote, and so we did. That Harper's Ferry
crew laughed and joked, confident as crows, boasting
as anybody would, even Deacon
Jackson in his grim and pious way: "Through
God's blessing," he dispatched to Lee, and isn't
that just how the Good Lord works? You never
know what He's doing, and just when most you're
satisfied He's on your side, look out, here
it comes. So Lee got Stonewall's message, knew
that within a day Jackson and the larger
half of his army could join him: he changed
his mind about retreat, thought the campaign
in Maryland was saved, looked at the high
ground behind Antietam Creek at Sharpsburg,
and said, "We will make our stand on these hills"—
and thus fulfilled again the ancient words,
The stouthearted are spoiled, have slept their sleep;
and none of the men of might have found their hands.
At thy rebuke, O God, both chariot and horse
are cast into a dead sleep. Surely
the wrath of man shall praise Thee.

*

Dunker Church, evening

That evening I sat in the Dunker Church

alone. Way off up cemetery way
the bump, bump now and then of our guns sounded,
and fainter, deeper, Yankee crews thumped back,
their heavy shot whistling toward that graveyard.
But birds still twittered in the trees around
the meeting house. It was just a square room,
as plain as biscuits on a clean-washed plate.
Against the north wall stood a bare table,
unpainted. On three sides, plank-backed benches.
The floorboards and plain benches gave the dry
rose smell of books a quiet schoolroom gives
in deep late summer, after months of heat
and standing empty in the afternoons.
The whitewashed walls bore no adornment but
the windows. What you see out such windows
looks more sharply colored for those white walls—
the clean walls, and that pure light of heaven—
green trees through hand-washed glass clearer than water—
and then some boys came in. They hushed at first
and then broke into talk and I stood up
and shuffled out. It was all right. I'd seen
what heaven is. I'd felt it in my lungs
and smelled it. This was what the great battle
was fought for. This is what we all wanted.
The battle's center was the Dunker Church.

Old Jack is Here

When General Lee drew up his line behind
Antietam Creek that early afternoon,
we hadn't but about fifteen thousand
worn-out, hungry, angry men. The Old Man stood

on Cemetery Hill, his hands still bandaged
from a fall, which must have made him just mad,
and looked across the middle bridge. He saw
the Yankee army, or half of it, forty
thousand, come down the Boonsboro Road, deploy
three miles along the Creek, place artillery—
some batteries of big twenty-pounders
included—on the high ground. McClellan
could have knocked us over with a strong sneeze,
but old Marse Robert knew he wouldn't. No,
say what you will about the vaunted Young
Napoleon, he was a coward through
and through. Still, they were nervous times. Later
on, some enterprising Yank division
commander shoved one brigade to our side
of the bridge, but they sat down and looked pretty.
It made some of our boys anxious, so when
old Stonewall showed up, a tuckered Johnny
caught sight of him on Cemetery Hill
confabbing with the Old Man; he ran back
to his company shouting, "It's all right
boys, Old Jack is here!" Such was the effect
old Stonewall had upon some boys. You knew
that Jackson being there meant Jackson's men.
He'd taken his entire Second Corps down
to Harper's Ferry; now they filled the road
behind him. All next day they'd be coming
in, and Young Napoleon in blue would
wait another day rather than attack
when inconvenient. Old Jack. It's hard
to say now what the Army thought of him.

He'd made a brilliant show all right that spring
down in the Shenandoah, defeated
a bevy of generals inept even
by Yankee standards, out-marched and surprised
them one after another and put scare
into the whole Yankee nation, Old Abe
included. But then he came to Richmond
with his Valley Army and disappointed
everyone: sluggish, slow as molasses
in January to attack, his mind
off somewhere, who knows, praying maybe, while
everyone else pitched in. But then brilliant
again, out-marching, outfoxing John Pope
at Manassas, his whole corps springing up
behind Pope's army; and then holding fast
while Pope attacked him. Jackson's boys stood all
day long, even throwing rocks when cartridges
gave out. It must have galled old Jack no end
finally to have to send for help. Longstreet
had arrived by then with the First Corps, but
held back—he was one cool fellow, Old Pete—
even telling Marse Robert No, not yet,
let Jackson hold his line a little longer;
we'll hit their flank tomorrow. And he did,
destroyed them, rolled them up, sent them running,
but by then Old Jack was down to the last
rind of his last lemon. It's hard to say
what Old Jack thought of Longstreet after that.
Old Jack was secretive. He rode a little
horse, too short for Jack's long legs, held a hand
up sometimes for his circulation's sake,

was a Presbyterian deacon—wouldn't
miss Sunday services to save his soul—
and it was said his eyes lit up in battle.
Old Blue Light, some called him. He loved fighting,
hated Yankees, loved his wife, loved children,
prayed to the God of Battles and to Jesus.
Some say he marched and killed his men without
second thoughts, spending like a drunken sailor;
others said he was the best of the best.
After he was gone, the war stopped going
well, is the plain fact, a plain fact that could
tell two different truths—one that he was missed, or
that all those men he spent were missed. He was
a little crazy maybe—good crazy
for a war, which is bald insanity
made visible. We are all half crazy
sometimes. I say we are all Longstreet men
or Jackson men at birth, but General Lee
was both—the Longstreet half the solid half,
the Jackson half a lunatic as brilliant
as the sun across a row of bayonets.
Say what you will, we needed Jackson's men
and what were they without Old Jack? What were
we all? One more thing—the reason General
Lee conferred with Old Jack and not Longstreet
was that the two had the essential thing
in common: they both were belligerent
beyond belief, which is to say that somewhere
each was mad as hell; and that is why we
all were there, why we rose up and defied
the whole damnyankee nation: sometimes you

just get mad as hell and there's nothing you
can do but fight. Honor demands you fight.
So Lee and Jackson waited for the sons
of bitches, and the sons of bitches came.

Army of the Potomac

Before the battle

The 15th of September was the last—
the ending of the world our God had made,
the final day of right and wrong as we
imagined it. The predictable past
should have crowded across the dusty stage
and we soldiers should have seen
all the seals between life and death breaking,
the pale horse steaming, God putting on rage.
The end had come. Everything would be changed
by bullets, by mistakes we were making,

by thirst, straggling, by lack of food and sleep;
every general's will would be shattered,
and every man's plans thrown after the deep
receding tide of the future. We marched
to seal the promise Mr. Lincoln made—
the promise to his God, the Unflattered,
the Truth in Himself, the One near and far,
to Whom the moody President had prayed,
learning prayer in the midst of civil war,
and the promise was the thing that mattered.

The promise would be proven on our pulses
and kept for the dead. He promised to free
their slaves, the South's hostages to fortune—
Jesus' children, three and a half million
mammys, field hands, servants, mistresses, split
families—to be given their justice:
liberty for the price of victory.
And there we were: entrusted with the Will
of God and didn't know it—a feeble
instrument for the Lord God Almighty,

and an uncertain vessel for that grand
man's discovery of what it all meant.
If it all came true, who could understand
the future?—in which God does a new thing,
speaks through a prophet invisibly sent
from Illinois, just as it is written
in Bible fairy tales—independent
of our institutions, laws: freedom rings
anew at last. God's word is spoken,
and by us the seventh seal is broken.

*

And it all came true. By evening we saw
the banks along Antietam Creek. We ate
our first in thirty-six hours. Our brigade
was down to eight hundred, for we had fought
three battles in two weeks. We lay down beside
high water, upstream at the Keedysville
Road. Its bridge still stands. Our dreams kept vigil

on the field where desire invades the mind
and fears challenge fears with sudden voices,
while someone somewhere made tomorrow's choices.

*

Little Mac

I'd take our Little Mack before their Lee.
He took good care of us, and our lives mattered.
Those are a soldier's reasons, not History's,
but put aside awhile what you have heard
about Mac's vanity and timidity.
Who hasn't faults? The vaunted General Lee
would fail to win in Maryland for two
bad reasons—reasons worse than tactical
mistakes, and less excuse. Arrogance you
can comprehend; it is a man's downfall.

Soldiers though we were, Lee didn't think we
could march or fight. Both times he crossed the River
he got surprised when Mr. Lincoln's army
marched fast to fight him. Wouldn't the man see?
What had we done but march and deliver
battle? We inferiors would nearly
destroy his damned army at Antietam
but his blind excuse would always be numbers.
Little Mac, no tactician, fought only
two-thirds of our men: we fought man to man.

And one more thing, if anyone wonders
these days: one-fourth of our men were green—boys
who hadn't fired a musket, couldn't load,

didn't know "oblique" from "fire by file," nervous
as butterflies: new regiments destroyed
at the first volley. We should have lost. Go
find how many colored folk came with us:
none. Lee brought thousands, not counted. We should
have been outnumbered. That is Reason Two:
General McClellan did what he could do

to feed and clothe us, keep our spirits up,
not waste our lives; but Lee didn't keep his
army intact. Half of his men gave up
the march—no shoes, no food, too little rest—
or never crossed the River at all. Lee
and Jackson wasted their men, but victories
made the deluded Rebs love them for it.
Generals in those times fought ten days a year:
beans and boots, not bullets, are what win wars.
Washington's Continentals didn't quit.

But people do not want to understand
war; they want diversion, romance. Battles
turn into books, and books are just pretend.
Who doesn't want to leave the life they live
and march with Lee, or leap into a saddle
to ride with Stuart? It is all make-believe.
Soldiers don't believe as much as survive—
eat, sleep, walk, sweat in the heat, breathe red dust,
shoot in the smoke, get sick, do what you must,
and the general's job is to keep you alive.

*

On the Smoketown Road

We crossed Antietam Creek at Pry's Mill Bridge
late in the day and marched in column west.
The little farms were worlds cut off by ridges
from each other, houses in hollows, crests
of low hills not offering much to see.
Very bad. Where there is no vision, soldiers
perish. The battle tomorrow would be
nothing but surprises: there woods and folds
could hide anything and even conceal
us from each other. The generals won't know

anything. It is the dreadful unknown
that quiets men marching to battle. Bold
fellows joke and deride and then fall silent
with the others, looking at the country
we might be seeing for the last time—trees
in late summer leaf, corn a man's hat high,
orchards weighed down with heavy green apples.
You know your soul is not your own, but still
you feel a grim nervousness inside, palms
sweat, and your mind fixes on scenes of home.

My mother would be standing at the stove
right then, suppertime, hands smoothing her apron—
or maybe she would go to the window
this time of day, thinking about her son.
I had a sister then, eighteen years old,
and still some faint freckles under her eyes
if she were out in the sun. Her new beau
was in my company; but I still got

more letters than he did. He was too shy
for her, but I watched him, and I thought.

We turned south, knowing we would find the Rebs
that way. It was a narrow lane, quiet
until we came through, quiet like a hot
summer evening when only the black flies
move, a humming, murmuring drone you get
used to and don't hardly hear. Skirmishers
way up ahead found them. We heard the *pop*,
pop of musket fire, becoming regular,
rising. In a half hour the column stopped
while a brigade ahead went back to war,

leaving the road to form line of battle.
It sounded like murmuring way up front,
musketry rose to a steady rattle,
and then the *boom*, *boom*-ing of heavy guns
from our batteries back where we had come,
then sharper, closer crashes front and right,
but it didn't last long. Our boys drove them.
We went on, then turned toward the setting sun,
then bivouacked in some woods for a cold night
of no fires, crackers; and lay on our arms.

Army of Northern Virginia

1st Texas

The woods behind the Dunker Church were far
from quiet at dawn. Hood's whole division
crowded in among the trees, sprawling, talking,
sleeping, making fires to cook the coarse flour
they were waiting for the Quartermaster
to unload. They hadn't eaten anything
but green corn and green apples for three days
or thereabouts, and I can tell you green
corn and sour apples aren't the best companions
on the march. They hurt your chompers
going in, and then run out as painful
as they went in, and quicker. The straggling
in the Army was due to poor diet—
some of the boys ran off to forage food;
the rest just didn't have the strength to walk.
But if I do say it myself, the men
who got to Sharpsburg were the best we ever
had, the ones who made it there. Those Texans,
now, the 1st Texas, set the woods alive
with murmuring, they and the rest of Hood's
Division, twenty-three hundred men all

told, plus servants and the men of other
brigades packed in there. Then, above their own
noise, the spattering rattle of muskets
drifted into the woods, then heavier fire,
and then that terrible concussing—guns
of Stephen Lee's battery and others
taking up the fire in front of the church,
right outside the woods, and then the Yankees
with their 20 pounders on the heights across
the Antietam, they thudded away. Soon
the odd shell or solid shot crashed through branches
like lumbermen felling hardwood. Heavy
limbs came down on men—and then the tearing
canvas sound of musketry not a thousand
yards away, like heavy cloth ripped inside
a cave, cloth a hundred yards long. The boys
from Texas made their cakes of flour as fast
as they could, knowing what was coming, knowing
they'd be called for, cooked without utensils,
spearing dough on bayonets and holding
it over their sputtering fires, angry
as hornets at the damnyankees for not
giving them a moment's peace to eat—then
our men running in bunches, black powder
griming their faces like bats out of hell,
crashing into the woods—and the long roll
sounded Assembly, To Arms, and the boys
scooped up their hot half-baked dough and crammed it
into their mouths while milling, stepping around
fires and other boys—"Company A here!"
"Company C, form up!" Law's Brigade, still

getting into line, scrambled and trotted
out of the woods, dodged between the pieces
and impatient crews, missiles screaming, plowing,
and Wofford's men, three Texas regiments,
one Georgia, one Palmetto, formed a line
across the Pike between the woods and Law.
On their far left the broken companies of Starke's
Brigade and others ran for the woods, smoke
all around, and then the Texas boys saw
what they were running from. A wide blue line,
more a string of gangs, came booming along
after them and straight toward the batteries
around the church. Hood's men, both brigades all
along the line a quarter mile long, raised
muskets, aimed, and on the order fired low—
a stunning thunderclap, and through the smoke
a man could feel the other line die, hear
them scream; and mounted officers could see
the blue devils stop, reel collectively,
half their line it seemed going down, but not
back—they stood and fired, and all of Hood's men
reloaded, bullets zip-zipping, smelling,
seeking, striking flesh, then another volley
and the officers rode through the lines forward
shouting "Charge! Give them Texas hell! Charge! Charge!"
And all the line went forward in a hurricane
of fox calls, high *yee-yip-yips,* long howls, ghostly
wolf moans—the Rebel Yell from two thousand
throats, raises one's blood better than whiskey—
the Texans, Alabamians, all the boys
together going forward. Those dark blue

uniforms just stood—black hats, that Black Hat
brigade, stood and fired and then they moved back,
some fast, some slow, some turning to fire, stubborn
sons of bitches, just a couple hundred of them,
but it took better men than Yankees
to hold Hood's boys—such men as never were
found on God's green earth, by God; and they moved
them. Lee said Texas boys always moved them,
and he knew whereof he spoke. The Texans
followed all the Yanks right into the cornfield,
what was left of it, half-stalks here and there
sticking up between men, bodies, blue, gray,
butternut, a streak of shot New Yorkers
in red pants. Left of the Pike a battery
bucked and roared, and shot crashed through the Texas
line, canister heavy and hot, screaming
shells exploding; on the ground all varieties
of Yankees, near the Pike those dark blue frock coats
and tall black hats, stepping on black hats everywhere
and there they were, halfway back in that field
forming line again and firing, a cut
of bullets sweeping through the Texas line,
the Texans mad as hell, and the 1st Texas
charges forward. Back behind their flank, guns
shooting fire. A whole brigade it seems like
of Yankees across the road crashing musket
fire down along Wofford's line—they turn, they
halt, they return fire, men falling, knocked down,
some running to the post-rail fence along
the pike to get at the Yankees across

the road—a Yank battery pulls lanyard
and whole rails fly back and men, not men but
parts of men, arms, haversacks, heads, muskets,
explode into the air, smoke, no more yells,
shooting every which way, everyone cursing,
shouting orders, privates and all, laughing
like the damned or mad, no colors standing,
wide-eyed men stumbling, dead men on the ground,
wounded crawling, smoke, crowding, shells, and then
everything is red, red like the middle
of the sunset, red air and red screams, red
powder smoke, and the smell, the sweet steely
odor of blood, rivulets, runnels, pools
on the trampled ground, men, muskets, knapsacks,
and in with everything pieces of cornstalks—
a flat litter of cornstalks all over,
leafy, split, and not one standing, and now
they're coming back, the 1st Texas, what's left
of them, no officers, just handfuls, groups,
two companies clean gone, shot every man,
the others down to a few. They'd gone
almost to the north fence of the cornfield,
going after those Wisconsin men, Black
Hats running now, clearing that fence, climbing
it and leaping, and all along that fence
a line of Pennsylvanians lay still,
their muskets resting on the bottom rail,
sighting under the smoke and when the Black
Hats went up over them they fired—all fired—
rising bullets of their Springfields killing
damn near all the Texas men at once, damn

near all of them, and hell if I'll try to
say more. Jackson asked General Hood, "Where
is your division, Sir?" and Hood said, "Dead
on the field."

Army of the Potomac

The Cornfield

It drizzled, I think it was most of the night.
The boys laid their knapsacks on their musket
locks, and on those pillows we tried to sleep.
If you did sleep before the coming fight
it was dozing, fitfully, cold and wet
and very unpleasant. You dreamed strange dreams,
memories jumbling with harsh noises, frights,
murmurings through the trees; a dozen times
you thought it was time, expected Assembly,
prayed maybe, prayed hard, imagining lines,

long lines of the enemy, bayonets,
coming on with their infernal high yell,
crashing with their red flags through summer wheat,
and then orders shouted and the long roll,
the boys all around groaning, on their knees,
getting up, orders to pile our knapsacks,
wet smell of trees, just enough light to see,
crowding through the woods into the open,
crowding into column, flags uncased,
Forward! Forward! Forward, Wisconsin men!

Their shells are crashing, blowing up in air,
screaming, then one strikes ahead of us, flashes
through a dozen men. The Brigade passes
while some boys get the wounded off, the dead
carried aside—a man staggers, no arms,
seems to be awake, silent, but half bled
to death already. Our boys will not scare.
General Gibbon halts us in a farmyard,
directs the colonels of the regiments
to redeploy, form lines, forward again.

Their skirmishers crouch all across the fields
and at the buildings of the farm ahead.
Two companies go forward charging them,
clear them out. Our lines are enfiladed
by Rebel batteries on a hill west
a quarter mile. We are in their plain sight.
You see smoke puffs, orange flares in the dawn light:
more guns a half mile straight ahead—the Rebs
crossing fire on us. This orchard's trees spray
when they're hit—all those limbs blown clean away.

We climb the orchard's fence. An open field
in clover, house and buildings, clapboards bright
in the sharp early sun—and a cornfield
straight ahead. You can see the gleaming lights
of bayonets in that field: graybacks waiting
there for us. The corn is higher than hats.
We go in, moving down the rows, bayonets
leveled; bullets clip through the stalks irate

for secession. "*Charge! Charge!*" We are running—
I want to get out from the corn—men falling

at my left knock me to my knees; stumble
forward, running, a grayback skirmisher
lies folded, I clear him and the stubble
ahead flies all directions—explodes—murder,
a line of infantry, the bastards—fire
back, load, the order "*Charge!*" Men behind me
press and we all go forward; cornstalks are cleared
away in front, shreds everywhere, you see
the sons of bitches moving back, turning
to fire but most of them just plain running.

We leap the cornfield's fence. Along with us
New Yorkers pitch and pile over the rails.
We start forward out of breath, but we run
in a rough line to keep up with our flags.
There's a small white church about five hundred
yards ahead, and those Rebel guns firing—
and hundreds of Rebs turn, new ones fall in—
a thousand graybacks volley and we're cut
like cornstalks, fall back to the fence,
rally on the colors, laugh crazy, shout

hoarse huzzahs, load like devils, fire without
aiming. Officers run along behind,
"Aim low boys! Give them hell!" There is no doubt
we give them hell—red flags are shot from color
bearers; their minie-balls were a hard wind
now dying down—go after them once more,

over the fence, and this time they are running
like rabbits, running like gray and brown hares—
and we walk after them. A field away:
the church and those guns. We have won the day.

The boys whoop. *It ain't MacDowell's army,*
you gentlemen! It's McClellan! We shout.
We fought our fight, and now we are fought out.
This was the Elephant. What we have seen
and what we have done is the worst fighting
anyone has ever seen. But forward,
forward to the church. Officers are righting
our line; and now it's after the cowards.
Two hundred yards is all that's needed now.
Out from those woods, look! Trotting into rows,

must be three thousand Rebels, new Rebels—
two dozen flags—Texas flags with one star,
and all their other rubbish flags, Rebels
by the thousands. How few of us there are.
We halt and load. We can hear their orders:
"Aim, boys! Give them—" Like a scythe their bullets
sweep across us, cut us down. We are murdered
on our feet—boys knocked backward, knocked down, sick
thunks of bullets hitting bone, hitting heads.
We walk backward, leaving the pasture thick

with our friends; and just then it seemed the earth
and sky reversed, tumbling together. Deaf
in a kind of silence I saw men's mouths
open shouting; everything tinged with red.

The men were backing, so many muskets
too hot or fouled. I couldn't ram the rod,
threw it down and picked another up, wretched
barrel fouled, ran to find another, blood
smeared on its stock, a man's trunk; we run back
to the shattered cornfield fence, the ground black

with bodies, here and there clusters of gray—
the corn gone—the place changed—cornstalks cut down
as if you'd pared them with a knife, shot away,
and smoke biting the eyes, stabbing the lungs,
the awful grit of powder on the tongue.
I pick up a good musket—I bend down
and smell blood, had smelled blood all along
but now I knew it. Shells plowed the dead; dying
boys tore at their coats and jackets, crying

for help or water as we ran. Ahead
in the smoky wreck a major shouted,
"Stand here! Stand here!" and we turned and loaded.
Before a dozen heartbeats, here came through
the smoke a Texas flag, slowly, waved side
to side by its bearer. We tired few
fed them our volley and tore a yards-wide
vacancy where those filthy colors were.
They charged us then, those gallant Texas men,
charged our two dozen, and we ran again.

We ran back to the fence where we'd started
seems like eternity ago, packed tight
with prone and kneeling men, and our scared hearts
never felt so wide and grateful to see

anyone our whole lives as those fighting
boys from Pennsylvania. We hit the fence
and pitched over, and their blessed volley
settled once for all the arrogance
of those Texans. We found them shot to rags.
But I let someone else pick up their flag.

Army of Northern Virginia

I wonder what a man is. Soil is soil
and soul is soul, and a man is soil and
soul. But where is the man? Not in the soil
and not in the air. I think man is fire:
man in war is fire; man in love is fire.
The difference between man and beast is fire.
I saw the dead. Their fire was gone. The soul
consumes man, consumes men—armies of man
after man—endlessly seeking its God
with whom the soul is in love and at war.
Man is the sun on earth, image of God.
My soul is among lions, and I lie
even among them that are set on fire.

Artillery Hell

When Stephen Lee's artillery dropped trail
on the plateau of the white Dunker Church
his gunners learned the meaning of "Artillery
Hell." McClellan's twenty-pounders across
Antietam Creek four miles away could reach
him, but three-inch rifles and Napoleons,
mere field artillery, could not strike back.

By high mid-morning, must have been eighty
Yankee rifles and Napoleons arced
from north to east, the Hagerstown Pike to
the Mumma farm, all plowing shot and shell
on Lee's fast-firing batteries in front
of that small white church. You've seen the picture,
the strange, still, "this-is-death" old photograph:
the six dead men, the shattered horse under
the caisson, scattered blankets, the post fence,
the church with shot holes, the pair of empty
shoes in front. Those men were us—clothes bursting,
dead faces sucking flies; those were my friends.
We came to settle up. I was those dead men.
They could have been artillery, but might
could have been Kershaw's infantry. We crossed
fire on Yankees in the Cornfield—Lee's guns
and Stuart's up on Nicodemus Hill;
and they crossed fire on us on this plateau.
The one man's leg looks to be missing: shot
or shell. But all the others look intact,
so I say infantry, Kershaw's Brigade.
Kershaw came running; Jackson sent them in
to strike that bare blue flank, that three-brigade
stupid blind death march pretty as you please,
that swept in from the east across the fields—
the Cornfield, the clover and grass pastures—
where the Yankee First Corps and Hood's Texans
had howled across an hour ago; must have
trod on lots of dead and wounded Yankees,
ours too—and came right into our West Wood
where Jackson threw McLaws' Division yelling

on their flank, Kershaw's Brigade among them.
Those boys shot Yankees by the barrel-full,
chased them running northwards out of the woods,
a-whooping and a-hollering, though tired
from fighting down at Harper's Ferry and
marching up to Sharpsburg in the night.
They ran the Yankees north, but Kershaw turned
three regiments east because something wrong
had happened by the church. Lee's guns had limbered
up and galloped out of there. All our guns
in front of the church were gone, had dashed off.
Some Yankee regiment or two had scared
them off, it must be. You didn't leave guns
in front of infantry unless support
was close at hand. I think artillery
could take care of itself, but the gunners
dreaded losing pieces more than anything.
—Let's punish them, those rash Yankees, attack
them, drive them off, so our guns can come back.—
The angry gray line yipped the Rebel yell
and surged across the Dunker Church plateau,
faces toward the sun. That plateau dropped off
a little on its eastern side, and there
a brigade of quiet Yankees waited
for our boys to show, waited until we
were seventy yards away, then rose up.
Their volleys wiped out companies of men.
Our flags went down and barely got carried
off. The shuddering line of butternut
and gray tried to stand and fire back, shot down
by dozens, scores, brave in terror and smoke;

but the only sensible thing was run,
and then they ran like hell, into the woods,
the Federals shouting that Hurrah like happy
Yanks can do, following our boys across
the plateau, past the church, into the woods.
There you have the difference; there you have
the war: the South tried to defend the Church,
the Yankees tried to seize it. It is writ,
"the kingdom of God is taken by force,
and the violent carry it away."
The Yankee battle line stayed in our woods
a good half hour, without support, two blue
brigades—didn't know the whole division
on their right was gone. But it was clean gone.
Eventually, we hit the Yankees hard
on both their flanks at once—how I'll never know—
both flanks were in the air and both stone blind
in those woods. Now it was the Yankees' turn
to run like the devil, hell following
after. There was no Yankee line to fall
back to until the East Woods, so they ran
across the whole morning's ruined battlefield,
out of the churchyard, across the turnpike,
and back across the devastated corn
with all its crawling, thirsty, shot-down men,
the smell of blood, the smell of blood and smoke,
and the ringing bell of terror—they ran
through it all and we shot them in their backs
as they had shot us down at the turnpike
two hours earlier, but we did not
follow this time. No charge was made across

those fields, following. Our left was played out.
We were nothing but rags and string and spit.
We'd done all men can do. But Old Jack wanted
to strike them again. He sent a boy up
a tree near the church to look how many
Yankees could be seen. The fields were uneven
so that you couldn't know what waited over
the rise in front of you. The field beyond
looked empty, but in between anything
could be there, as we had found to the sorrow
of many and many a sad Southern
home. The boy exclaimed, "Hooee! There's oceans
of 'em, Ginral!" "Just count the flags, Sir! Count
the flags!" So up there where the enemy
could see and shoot him, the climber counted
out loud, deliberate as a pachyderm,
and Jackson steel-eyed, grinding his teeth, standing
under the tree until at thirty-nine
he barked, "You may come down, Sir!" At two flags
each regiment, that would make four or five
new Yank brigades, two divisions maybe;
where they came from only the Good Lord knew.
So much for an attack. Would have been like
throwing handfuls of our goober shells against
a wall. Old Jack was mad, Marse Robert too,
but what did that matter? We were all mad;
the whole damn South was mad as hornets. Why
else would we have fought that everlasting war?
Why do you think we crossed the Potomac
into Maryland?—to impress the French?
To charm Great Britain into backing us?

To lift the despot's heel from Carroll's shore?
We went there after the Yankee army,
to kick the sons of bitches in the head
one last time, one final time, to kill them
in great enough numbers this time where they
couldn't get away; to make the vermin
leave us alone finally. If you think
the war was about anything else, then
I guess you never heard the Rebel yell.

Army of the Potomac

General Mansfield is killed

The Twelfth Corps went in close behind the First,
packed in dense columns, not in battle lines,
the worst formation possible: one burst
of a shell, or one solid shot's blind flight
could murder and maim a score of good men.
But six of its regiments were brand new,
in uniform three weeks; and, poorly led,
its veteran brigades had been marched raw,
surprised, and routed in the Shenandoah—
they surely dreaded a surprise again.

So their corps commander wouldn't have them spread
out. Mansfield, a biblical forty years
in the Army, didn't trust volunteers
under fire. He went by the Book, which he'd read
at West Point years ago, for until two
days past, he had never been in the field.
He had walked among the troops, the undrilled
and seasoned, firm and reassuring—knew
them all, they felt. He looked like God: white beard,
flowing white hair; he was both loved and feared.

His Twelfth Corps formed a dense half mile across
the First Corps' rear, the left behind the woods
west of the Cornfield. Mansfield himself led
forward a new regiment who seemed lost
without him, the 128th PA.
The men willing, earnest, but ignorant
of commands their officers shouted, went
into line where Mansfield pointed them, brave
under their commander's eye. They began
firing their new rifles. "They're your own men!"

Mansfield shouted, wrong. "You're shooting your own
men!" But Rebels in the smoky West Woods,
canny and practiced, and not Union men,
had got the new boys and the General good.
The General realized that he had guessed
wrong—and then took a bullet in the chest.
The boys nearby saw him shudder, then reel,
then like an immortal slowly dismount.
He led his horse a few steps, then he fell.
Transfixed Pennsylvanians gathered around:

the General lay hatless, face turned aside
against the ground, blood flowing from his mouth.
This was the only general they had known.
The soldiers' universal faith had lied,
and now they knew that they were on their own.
Their colonel led them back and faced them south,
and then was shot to death in front of them.
A colonel from another regiment

rode over, sent back for several sergeants,
and got them into battle line again.

All the while those men were taking fire
from Rebels in the woods, across the fields,
and from the massed artillery placed high
on Nicodemus Hill. Good sense required
they move before they broke. The order "Charge!"
was shouted—one word they could understand—
and with relief enraged by grief they charged,
imperfectly, a ragged line, each man
wide-eyed, determined, sweaty hands tightly
gripping muskets; slow, steady, a mighty

tide of blue with supports at either side—
the sight of which caused Hood's right regiments
to fall back from the cornfield's eastern edge—
this flesh and blood tide of innocents.
Another Reb brigade was waiting for them
south of the Cornfield, and when the blue line
came sweeping from that bloody stubble field
they stood and fired. The crash, the zipping whine
of bullets, buck and ball, the flashing shells,
the smoke, smell of blood, cursing, yelling, screams,

were too much for the untried brave to brave,
and the shocked, confused survivors fell back
disordered, some men running hard to save
themselves, blank-eyed and thoughtless as jackrabbits;
others walking backwards, refusing to run—
all the 128th back to where General

Mansfield had ridden out and lined them up.
Others in the ruined and writhing Cornfield
stayed and fought, insanely devoid of fear—
Rebel yells, solitary Union cheers.

*

Greene's Division takes the East Woods

Old George Sears Greene—his hair was white as Mansfield's
but otherwise he was one tough general—
his division marched right through the East Woods
and gave the Rebels a taste of real hell.
The woods were ours, and would be from then on.
The General reformed his lines and waited
for orders to advance. Meanwhile on both
sides of him two Second Corps divisions
came up: French's on the left, as if fated
for the Sunken Road, would attack due south;

and Edwin Sumner, another white-haired
general, commanding the Second Corps,
put Sedgwick's division on Greene's right, rode
with Sedgwick, marching westward unprepared:
the three brigades in broad lines one behind
the other, no skirmishers ahead, no
flankers fanning out beside, bold and blind
across the Cornfield into the West Woods.
To be right's not enough if you're a soldier;
it's not enough to be brave, true, and good:

you must be lucky, and not be led by fools,
brave or otherwise. On Sedgwick's far left

the untrained Philadelphia Brigade,
uniformed like French North African troops—
fezzes, baggy trousers, short jackets—new
to marching in close order and unused
to rifles, officers' commands, untested
by the Rebel Yell, received the enfilade
fire first: a thunder crash, a thousand bullets
cutting through them, the air all hissing blades.

Next year at Gettysburg some of these men
would stand, the bravest men on any field,
a thin blue line awaiting Pickett's Charge;
but here it seemed half of them were shot dead
or wounded, and the rest simply stampeded
northward, a dense Rebel line hitting them edge-
on and rolling up, arcing around them
west, south, and east. Sumner had been foolish
but now was brave as a wounded lion,
riding to his left into the fire, cool

and enraged, bellowing, waving, leading
out the stunned new regiments—all three lines
crumbling now, crushed and routed and streaming
up across the Miller farm toward the North
Woods. The Rebels followed, in their turn blind,
yahooing, chasing for all their worth—
and George Greene's battle line crashed into them
and sent the Rebels back into their woods.
He'd followed Sumner, aligned on his left,
and drove toward the church. Old George Greene was good.

His two brigades scattered all the Reb guns
firing from the Dunker Church plateau, crashed
into Kershaw's South Carolinians
jubilantly whooping after Sumner,
and pushed through the smoky, moaning backwash
of the Rebel flank attack, Yankee cheers
filling the East Woods now, Greene's line farther
than any Union troops into the Rebel
left center. But they were alone. The whole
of Sumner's corps was gone. An officer

of Sumner's found Greene, asking "Didn't you know?"
George Greene's reply was loud and eloquent
and sulphurous in the extreme. Back he went
with his two brigades, but stopped on the plateau
to hold out there as long as he could, white
Dunker Church in front of his lines, the goal
of all the morning's fighting, seized and let go
twice, three times now, all three Union corps fighting
into its yard, for a day in thy courts O Lord
is better than a thousand. But lightning

flashed and thunder rolled, and a voice said Not
yet, Not yet O Man, for thy blood must pour
'til every drop drawn by the lash begets
its drop drawn by the terrible swift sword.
And on Green's left there was no help, for back
in the West Woods, dim general French emerged

and saw a Rebel line straight to the south,
not west where Greene had gone, so French attacked
what he could see—a vision blurred and cursed—
and ran into the Sunken Road, the dragon's mouth.

Army of Northern Virginia

The Sunken Road

We settled in the Sunken Road like rustling
leaves, butternut and brown and grays of all
description, filling that dog-elbowed road
with two understrength brigades: Anderson's
and Rodes's. They were good men, full of grit,
wiry and hungry and angry enough
to kill and die. The whole Army at Sharpsburg
was the best we ever had—angry men
who survived and stayed. Marching and hunger
shook off the tender-footed, tender-hearted,
cowardly, and otherwise unfit. We
were the raw bones and nerve, the beating heart,
of the Confederacy. We knew why
we were there; and you'd have to kill us first,
before we'd give up our rights, the rights we
were born with, and the rights we would die with.
Rodes's Alabamians on the left,
North Carolinians on the right, each
state on the field of battle somewhere, all
with their own friends and neighbors, sons, brothers,
cousins; we all understood each other.

Though not always in speech. The Louisiana boys
talked Creole; and boys from deep back-country
Mississippi talked like their own black folk,
parts of words away on leave and the rest
stuck together like molasses; Virginians
if not careful sounded half like Yankees
to the rest of us. There weren't many
mountain people, true lost mountain people,
who talked as though they'd just got off a boat
from England back in sixteen-something. Only
ones didn't talk with an accent of some
sort or other was the fellows from my
county. Well, wherever the boys came from,
we all sounded like home. We didn't sound
like machines, the way the Yankees did, clipped
and sharp and crisp and dry—just like machines
would talk if they could talk. And they would get
to the point right away, wouldn't they? If
some Yank were telling this here, the battle
for the Sunken Road would be done already,
the dead soaking the ground with their blood, and
we'd be moving on to Gettysburg, or
maybe even Appomattox, as if
life were always what's ahead, instead of
now, or instead of what it was back then,
in days gone by sunny and warm, settling down,
drifting down into memory like
leaves. You have to put value on what is,
love and respect what was, because that is
who and what you are; and that too is why
we were there, at Sharpsburg, and what we were brave

for. The Yankees just didn't understand
the South, never will, and that is why they
came blue line after blue line, and is why
we stood and shot them down. Our boys piled rails
up on the forward bank of the road, rails
from fences the good farmers of Maryland
would not miss at that particular moment,
nor begrudge their liberators in need.
The men stood in that low road three or four
deep, the front rank kneeling and leaning against
the forward slope. Officers gave orders
not to fire before they shouted the word,
and don't expect that word to come until
the Yankee battle line appears atop
the little crest ahead—not just their flags
and bayonets, but wait 'til you can see
the cartridge boxes on their belts, and aim
at those. It got so quiet then. You heard
Yank officers clear as could be across
two hundred yards of grassy field behind
that crest in front of us: "Fix bayonets!"
and "Keep even there, you men!" Green new troops
it must be, coming. And now you heard the tramp,
tramping, not steady but all at once, coming,
and our officers real quietly say,
"Steady, boys," say, "Hold your fire," real evenly,
and you'd swear you felt the ground trembling. Tramp,
tramp, tramp. An eagle shows above the crest,
then the flags, the Stars and Stripes, the state flags,
and then the bayonets. "Steady, gentlemen."
You see the caps and faces, blue jackets

and buttons down the front—your heart stops—cartridge
boxes—"Fire! FIRE!" You hardly hear the crash,
the thunder-clap: our flames and smoke shoot out
to them and cover everything. Our officers
standing up behind and above us shout,
whoop, order "Load, boys!" And through the smoky
air we see their whole front line, nearly all
of them, have gone down, are lying, crawling,
or running back—shot dead blue bodies down
along a line as far as you can see
in both directions. You ram the cartridge
down the barrel. Bodies lying in front of the crest
in a line, new blue uniforms: the first
volley's always the worst, because there's no smoke.
You can see to aim. There is smoke everywhere
now. Their line is all smoke. They are lying
down behind the crest, firing at us now,
minie balls past and through us, here and there
a striking sound like hailstones on the rails
in front of us. Up to the left a Yankee
color bearer lumbers back with his flag,
big as a cow. We have no fat men; they
are well-fed, these new Yanks, just wait—crashing
volleys, carefully aimed into the smoke.
Why aren't we getting struck more than we are?
Eighty yards, seventy—you set the sight.
The new Yanks must be shooting at the sky,
or if they're new recruits they close their eyes.
Our officers tell us to choose our man;
we'll need our ammunition by and by—
and sure enough, another line comes up.

And all new dark blue uniforms, against
the bright sky behind them, they are a line
of dark automatons with shining knives.
"Go back, you black devils!" we shout at them.
"Black devils! Get back, black devils!" Think what
you will—that we saw eight generations
of our servants rising up, apparitions
marching on to serve some righteous sentence
on us; but if you had been in that road,
you'd have seen devils, black or otherwise.
The Yankees were all conscience and no heart,
all conscience and no soul. What else were they?
Devils have no hearts or souls. We were right
to hate them; we were proper to hate them.
Listen to me this one time: Anyone
who kills for an idea has no soul.
The Yankees were the kind of people who
defend a thought at any cost, who put
ideas above human people—brothers,
sisters, sons, and mothers, kill them all
before you surrender that idea,
whatever it is—Union, equality, no matter,
they all sound good, sound right. Why else
did they come down to kill us? Why couldn't
they just leave us alone, when all we wanted
was to be left alone? Why not let us go?
Why not like Pharaoh, Let my people go?
We meant no harm to them. But to defend
a sacred formula they'd kill us all,
and kill our wives and sons and daughters too,
before they'd give up their idea. Why else

did they come down to subjugate our South,
when we were no threat at all to them,
offered no destruction on them, would leave
and go our way and mind our own affairs?
What business did they have with us? And all
of them no doubt felt sanctioned by Holy
Scripture, that book we use to kill
our fellow child of God on this earth. They say
the Bible is God's word, and yes I know
we used it too, our preachers did: inerrant
books are used to justify anything
that you do in their name. "Inerrant" tells
the world that we don't make mistakes. Use God's
authority to back you, and you have
no need to listen to that troublesome,
afflicted, sore, and agonizing heart,
but only to cold conscience. We Rebels
had heart. What else could we do but fight them?
They would never let up, those Yankees. We
tried their Congress, tried reason, tried patience:
they left us nothing to do but defend
ourselves. And they wore us down. I am worn
with arguments. A Southerner defends
his sacred rights. We were Southerners. Let
that be enough.
            The second Yank brigade
charged us three times—or tried three times to break
over that crest; and each time we poured fire
at them so good it was a sin, until
they also took to Mother Earth. They nor
their first brigade broke and ran, as they should

have done; they stayed and shot it out with us.
And then a third brigade came up beside
the two, adding their fire. The road was hell.
I'll tell you later about Anderson,
but Rodes's Alabama boys faced twice
their number. Granted our boys had position,
and the Yankee boys were green, but I said
that road dog-elbowed. It was no angle
proper, just a bend, but Yankee ingenuity
at last discovered they could shoot across
to left and right, down the road where it bent.
The Sunken Road was filling up with dead—
ours. And then two veteran Yank regiments
rushed at the far end, broke into it, fired
where Anderson's boys were stacked close as peas.
Defense at times becomes a trap. And then
confusion served to wreck what might have been
retrieved. Rodes ordered his right regiment
to bend its flank and face the firing Yanks,
but its colonel thought he meant retreat. Next
to him, another colonel shouted, asking
if the order was for all of them to leave.
"Yes, all of us," the first one called, or so
the story goes. Sometimes you justify
catastrophe with sensible inventions.
In any case, things went as badly up
the road where Anderson's men stood in fire.

Army of the Potomac

The Sunken Road

Now General William French was the wrong man
in the wrong place at the wrong time—just where
the Good Lord wanted him, you understand.
His division had been thrown together
one day ago, to be precise; and seven
of its ten regiments were new recruits:
didn't know how to load and fire, and learned
in front of the Rebels; could march straight ahead
and that was all. The bravery of Union
youth, in love with something, with that Union

the Rebels hated—the war was simply
love and hate, so it was a civil war—
that bravery was what the future relied
upon, so it seemed. That's what bravery's for.
But bravery can be wasted, poorly led.
It all comes down to courage in the end,
not mere bravery, that and the Will of God,
strange and unknown, both terrible and good.
In this case that Will ran through a bloated
alcoholic, a gross fat man devoted

to his pleasures, red of nose, a man more
French than his name. But William French couldn't
have been all bad, because a dozen years
before, a young subordinate got sorely
indignant about some things French shouldn't
have been doing—the righteous have large ears,
and eyes made to search out iniquity—
and raised a charge of moral turpitude,
a charge French escaped but only barely.
And who was that young, self-important prude?

Thomas Jonathan Jackson, Old Stonewall,
himself a vessel of God's Will—though none
of us is used the way we like, and all
of us seem to learn too late that someone
else is God. There stood Jackson, a stone wall
mortared with impenetrable belief,
too righteous to be good, holding his line
on the Rebel left but only barely:
French could have broken him, supporting Greene,
but attacked the Rebel center squarely.

God meant the Rebel army to survive
that day, for some vast, brooding purpose. Why
else was French commanding where anyone
else would have followed Sedgwick, Sumner, Greene,
right toward the Dunker Church? French avoided
churches instinctively perhaps, and thus
became God's humble, drunken Instrument.
He saw a Rebel line behind the deadly

Sunken Road, and made his blind, bumbling thrust
there; and where the fool ordered, his men went.

You can't see God's Will; it is a sunken road.
Weber's Brigade formed battle line and marched
unseeing upwards toward the crest that over-
looked the old farm lane. Several hundred yards
wide, the line walked forward stately, eager,
terrified, cut through now by Rebel shells—
first their flags, then caps visible to Rebels
packed closely three deep beside each other—
then their belts at seventy yards, then "*Fire!*"
A sheet of flames, smoke, bullets: brave men fell

the length of Weber's line. It seemed that all
the men in front were struck. And brave men charged
again, and again, that murderous wall
of bullets; and then it was that courage
took over, with prudence: the men lay down
just behind the crest—Weber's and the two
other brigades, and there those green men stayed.
They stayed two hours, shooting, being shot, two
full hours or more at eighty yards, the brave
learning dull courage in that longest day

of their lives, those who survived, when the sun
stood still over the Sunken Road, and blue
uniformed bodies covered the high ground
and the road filled up with bleeding Rebels.
Courageous men know there's nothing to do
but stand the fire—or that is what we call

courage, that disciplined insanity
that makes all other virtues possible.
Courage is a willingness to bleed

that is a cousin of despair, a rage
that places you outside of your own brain,
a faith without a God, a loverless
love. Surely Lord God Jehovah poured men
toward the Sunken Road when the universe
was born, and we have marched the Sunken Road
since Moses parted the waters covering
it, and now we have arrived. Here we are:
the sun stands still at noon, directly over
us; our shadows fall on ourselves.
The road to glory is a road in hell.

Army of Northern Virginia

Anderson's Brigade was right of Rodes—
that's G. B. Anderson, not Richard, whose
division should have reinforced the road
but did more harm than good eventually.
George Anderson was wounded in the foot
right at the outset, like Achilles dying
finally from the wound. His wife and children
watched him fill up with poison back down South,
them nursing him. The bullet that hit him,
standing up behind the Sunken Road, far
enough behind to see his regiments
from end to end—exactly where he should
have been—that bullet might was meant for some
man's head down in the road. The fire was awful
there: not only musket fire but shells dropped
in from time to time, or burst overhead,
the boys packed down behind piled rails or stone
fences farmers built to keep their milk cows
from getting in the road. The ground was pasture
in front of Rodes and half of Anderson,
with a plowed field in front of our far right.
And have I mentioned how hungry our boys
were that morning? General Rodes himself ate

only one roasted ear of corn beforehand.
It seemed the sun stood still. The Yankees stayed
and fired as if they meant to stay 'til hell
froze over, and we'd stay that long ourselves.
You Yanks can kill us all, we thought; and then
our wives and sisters will fight you. The shrieks
of wounded men were constant as the roar
and rattle of the musketry. General
D. H. Hill that morning got his wish: dead
Yankees by the acre; but he also
got a thousand dead and wounded
Southern boys. I know some officers left
our line unbidden, but not many; more
were killed and wounded. For a fact, of forty
captains in George Anderson's brigade, two
got out unhurt. When Anderson went down,
a man named Phillips took the word to Colonel
Tew, the 2nd North Carolina—shouted
through the smoke and din that Tew commanded
the whole brigade now. Tew, a gentleman,
removed his hat and bowed to Phillips, showing
he had heard and thanking him for running
through the fire—and took a bullet right through
his head, temple to temple. The force blew
the Colonel's eyes out of his face. He was
a scholar, Colonel Tew. His sickened, furious
men laid him against the road bank, alive
somehow. He still gripped and pulled at his sword
when Yankees poured into the road two hours
later. Then Phillips ran back for Colonel Parker
of the 30th, ducking down the road,

and as he got to him a bullet struck
Phillips' head, not killing him quite; another
hit Colonel Parker, carved a valley through
the side of his skull, not killing him either,
but you could see the pulsing gray membrane
of the brain. So the brigade was leaderless
and fought regiment by regiment, or
company by company. When new troops
came up—Georgians and Floridians—no
officer could keep the new and old men
sorted out. Men shouted orders, but you
had no idea which were yours. Still we
stood in that road, firing our way, not like
Yankees—maddened and fast—but slow and cool,
like we were hunting varmints in the woods.
The Second Regiment fought with their poor,
mutilated colonel lying right there
in among them. Two days later, he still
lay there. There is a photograph of him
in that road. I have come to think photographs
of dead men are devices of the devil,
for God means soldiers to be buried, at least
to decompose, and not be shown in such
indignity forever. But might could
be if folks back home saw what soldiers see,
they wouldn't let the politicians start
wars. I don't know. I expect if photographs
are bad, war is worse, anyhow. If good
can come of indignity, let it be.
There is no indignity like a war,
and nothing more noble and heroic.

You should have seen how the boys stood. Companies
almost were wiped out, some of them, before
the Yanks got in on our right. We should have
held them. Wright's Georgians should have come in right
of Anderson, not up into his lines,
confusion reigning then I can tell you,
and to make it worse, those Georgians attacked—
charged right through Anderson like some damn fools,
and got shot by the score and came running back
and kept on running right on through the road.
It maybe wouldn't have got out of hand
if Dick Anderson, commander of that
division, hadn't also been wounded
right at the outset, with command falling
to some smart lawyer who didn't know beans
about military command. Decency forbids
I mention his name, but he got broke down
to private after Sharpsburg. Then General
Wright, who had this pious horse would always
kneel to drink—so much for piety—just
as Wright is riding forward with his men through
that corn, a shell penetrates the horse's
chest in front and bursts, blood and horse everywhere
and they said General Wright was thrown upward
like a doll a dozen feet, then stands up
and lurches forward and orders "Charge! Charge!"
to anyone who'll hear, and then they carry
him off the field. Some said he was drunk, but
that's just how Georgians talk. Colonel George Jones
of the 22nd Georgia took command,
but he was detested by all including

Wright and as if we had an excessive
quantity of officers, his own men
shot him—so some say. In any case he
was shot in the head and shot through a lung,
and that was how things went for us. Georgians
and Florida boys charged and retreated,
the rest of Anderson's division mixed
into the line in the road; and then one
hot-head Mississippi regiment fired
at the backs of our own men down in there.
Two regiments ran after five minutes.
In fairness one must say that Florida
lost seventy percent, and Georgia sixty—
nothing but sheer murder and confusion
everywhere, and if there weren't insanity
enough, some boys who charged those Yankee Irishmen
saw some bruising Molly behind their line
huzzahing and swinging her bonnet, mad
and reckless as could be. Makes you wonder
what's left to happen in this world. And then
those Yankee regiments slithered around
our right, so there you had sheer destruction.
You know, if there was one thing said on our
side worth keeping, it was what one fellow
wrote home: "The battle at Sharpsburg wasn't
the victory they claim it to be." After
our victory in the Sunken Road we ran
back through the corn and orchard and nothing
should have stopped the Yankees, but they never
came. And in that thousand feet of Bloody Lane
we left a thousand men dead, wounded, captured.
I reckon that we held them long enough.

Army of the Potomac

We had a fighting general that day.
Israel Richardson, "Fighting Dick," as good
an officer as wore the uniform—
either uniform—intelligent, brave,
a Vermonter and no nonsense, in no mood
to let the Rebels slip back South: he stormed
the Sunken Road on French's left. Meagher's
Irish Brigade uncased their emerald
flags with bright gold harps beside the Stars
and Stripes; Brooke's Brigade and the coward Caldwell's

deployed behind the Irish. Meagher was drunk
but full of fight, of course; rode his tall white
horse forward with his men. Down in the Sunken
Road the graybacks waited. The thunder-strike
of their first volley tore the Irish down
by regiments; five minutes of murdering
destroyed half the brigade. Colors went down.
"Raise the colors! Follow me!" Meagher's ringing
Irish tenor stirred another charge—and down
he went, horse shot. The Irish hugged the ground

like French's men, and now the Bloody Lane

roared like one long thunder, smoke in gray scuds
steaming everywhere, causes gone insane
and thirsty for the other cause's blood,
the plateau and the road pooled with fresh blood—
the cornfield behind the lane full of Rebel
reinforcements coming through, cannons flaming
silently it seemed in that immense roar—
bullets searing air, a hot random hell;
God walking in the smoke, calling, naming

those chosen to be hit, those smashed by shot,
those with throats ripped ragged by minie balls,
the man whose severed arm spins up and falls
on trampled meadow, whose unbuttoned guts
will pop loose purple and gray today, men
unlucky in God's providential plan,
whose children would run away from their prayers
if this thunder would break over their heads,
even if they knew tomorrow's rank dead
would be someone's fathers and brothers—theirs.

Through this steam and stew stalks Israel Richardson,
his face black as thunder, drawn sword flashing
in his hand. "Caldwell!" he roars to anyone.
"Where's Caldwell?" That brigadier is watching
from behind a haystack, someone finally
tells Fighting Dick. "Damn the field officers!" he
shouts, and sends Caldwell's regiments in himself.
Colonel Francis Barlow takes two regiments
around the Irish left, drives in the Rebel
flank, and crowds his charging, musket-clubbing men

into the Sunken Road at its far right
and blazes volleys down the Reb-clogged lane.
The Fifth new Hampshire, Colonel Cross, fights
into the road, and Rebels all the way
across the Irish front are slain in piles,
dead falling on dead, survivors barely
able to push out from the mass, climbing
into the cornfield. Now Richardson's
men rush the road, shoot, club, capture stunned
Rebels, and keep going, into the corn, blind

to what awaits them there—a battle line,
artillery, or nothing but running
graybacks? The Fifth New Hampshire in the road
is charged by a yelling Reb battle line
but Colonel Cross, a bandana tied around
his wounded bald head, his beard dirty red,
detests the yipping Rebel Yell, commands
his men to whoop like Indians. Union
men raise the war cry, hair-raising high screams,
and show the Rebs they aren't afraid of them.

The Rebel counter-charge was beaten back
and now Richardson knew there was nothing
left of the Rebel center. An attack
straight ahead right now, and both Rebel wings
would crumple like stuck spiders. The General
ordered a halt, hurried back and forth giving
orders to get back into line, was calling
a battery up for support—and a shell,
a Rebel shell, exploded next to him.

We were not meant to win.

That coward Caldwell was next in command.
No orders came from anywhere. Not from
division, corps, or from the high command.
The Rebels were beaten; but it would go on.
We should have crushed their left, we could have pierced
their center, and later that afternoon
their right should have been drowned in the river.
Sometimes it is good to be a soldier,
only a soldier. Were we blessed or cursed?
It is for others to make sense of it.

Afternoon. The Rohrbach Bridge

McClellan thought the enemy brought ninety
thousand men at least, plus cavalry and guns,
though how he thought the graybacks could supply
that many remains a dark conundrum.
The battles that summer around Richmond
must have convinced him the Rebels had hordes
of fanatical men, the way they poured
attacks at us for seven days. Believing
that, or at least desiring to deceive
himself, he could have done a good deal worse.

It's a wonder he attacked at all. Corps
after corps he ordered in, only one
in reserve. But why keep all of his horse
with him? That cost us the battle. Not one
company of cavalry was sent down

Antietam Creek to look for fords. Did he
save them for a *coup de main*? Abe Lincoln
said the whole army was Mac's bodyguard.
It must have been true for the cavalry
that day. If Little Mac had found a ford

to turn the Rebel right, instead of waiting
for Burnside to force through the Lower Bridge,
the Ninth Corps would have come up on the ridge
that was Lee's flank, twelve thousand strong. Delay
meant Lee could strip his right to reinforce
his left all morning. Finally only
three Rebel regiments guarded the bridge.
It was enough to keep us back for hours.
Bad as it sounds—twelve thousand infantry
held off by a minuscule Rebel force—

remember that the creek was four feet deep,
the banks on both sides bare and steep,
and army shoes are smooth as window-glass.
To wade the current, slow as in a dream,
was more than any officer could ask
his men when five hundred practiced killers
were posted on the other bank in trees,
behind a stone fence, and in rifle pits,
waiting for someone to stick up his head.
That bridge cost us a good one hundred dead.

The first two attacks failed. Men ran along
the lane that paralleled the creek two hundred
yards, exposed to fire—a shooting gallery

for Southern marksmen.
The cornfield and that ro
the West Woods swallow
machine, and still nothin
That corps wasn't actuall
for to make a long ugly st
Mac sent half Old Burn's

earlier, and like the profe
soldier and complete jacl
Burnside, master of the c
slowed everything down
Burnside didn't understa
were depending on this war to get their
killing done on time. I would say of all
the fools we had that called themselves generals,
Burnside was the worst. Now some men will swear
by Mac, but I will stick to Burnside—call

me faithful to a fault, but I am true.
You must allow some angry words in my
own way. We should have whipped them. We all knew
that once again the braggarts got away
because our generals were inferior
to theirs—the ones in high command, that is—
Burnside, Sumner, some say Mac himself. Our
men were as good as theirs, maybe better
for the shame and downright perseverence
suffered and shown forth in freedom's defense.

It now neared one o'clock. Two regiments—

Handwritten note: Stonewall p. 69 "Dead Yankees by the acre"

both fifty-firsts, New York and Keystone State—
were ordered out to rush the bridge. The men
had been deprived of their whiskey of late
and one of them spoke up: "Will we receive
our whiskey if we take the bridge?" "You will,
by God!" their general swore. And now you see
the role of little things in history.
That promise did the trick: they got their fill
after the battle—all of those who drank,

that is—and should have won the nation's thanks
for making possible a victory.
But incompetence and delay closed ranks
against us once again. Those regiments
ran down the hill and lined the bank—
the right, upstream, the Pennsylvania men;
the left, New York—and opened up a fire
on them so hot and fast and furious
the graybacks left their pits and scrambled higher
up the hill, and then our boys made their rush.

Oh, it was beautiful! The color guards
ran first onto the bridge, the Stars and Stripes
and state flags in front and angled forward
as four abreast, Keystone men on the right,
New Yorkers pouring in beside, a current
bluer and stronger than the Antietam—
shells bursting over them; our boys hurrahing
from the ridge and by brigades moving down
toward the stream, the Rebel gents on the run
full tilt now, and we're on the other side.

Once across, we shouldn't have been denied
the road to Sharpsburg. It wasn't too late
at one o'clock to get behind Lee's right.
It makes one furious enough to cry:
for what, exactly, did all those men die
at the bridge, if we weren't going to move?
What did all those sacrifices prove?
Burnside was the worst general of the war:
he used two hours to get his divisions
into line. Then the ever faithful Sons
of Liberty marched forward to slaughter.

Army of Northern Virginia

They take the bridge

Now tell me if I am in error here:
five hundred Georgians held the Rorhbach Bridge
'til kingdom come, for all practical purposes,
against twelve thousand Yankees. I reckon
those to be the bona fide numbers?
With all due modesty, I must conclude
that one true Southerner is worth a sight
of Yanks. Those Georgians finally withdrew
only for want of ammunition, which
our friends the Boys in Blue had in abundance.
We had position on them. We looked down
onto that bridge from an old stone quarry
on the hillside, and we filled out with men
shinnying up trees like they'd be going
turkey shooting; and then there was that stone
wall. Our guns in the cemetery up
behind the left covered the bridge just fine,
and took the Yanks under fire the moment
their officers prodded them off their ridge.

It was Christmas and turkey shoot in one.
You didn't have to move; all that you did
was choose which lumbering bluebelly you
wanted, and plug him. You got one every
time. You know those damn fools carried sixty
pounds on their backs, plus their rifle-muskets,
and of course their ammunition, which they
had to burn, and showered on us profligately.
You can't separate a Yank from his baggage.
Although the last delegation to charge
the bridge left their knapsacks up on the ridge
and ran down like demons. That was unlike
Yanks. The only thing I can figure is
that they were promised whiskey.

Army of the Potomac

General Rodman falls

A battle is no different from the life
we all observe and live, except we see
the terrible face of fatality
and it takes place in one very short time.
That which we will not conceive or admit
occurs to all. War is mortality
compressed; all doctors and preachers know it.
All patients die, and the congregation
is a regiment falling one by one.
War is life, and peace is a short respite.

But if God rules this flaming universe,
this God of vengeance and of battles Who
made us, and somehow justifies the curse
that falls upon us all, then I say who
understands anything? Those say they do
are the least wise, and use their holy books
to make a god's infallibility
their own. Battle teaches humility.
Whoever in this life does what is good
relies only on the heart's certainty.

There was a man named Martin Eakle, who
drove onto the battlefield that early
afternoon with horse and carriage: drove to
a grimy, sweating, thirsty battery
exchanging fire with the enemy.
The gunners were astonished, but the man
stepped down and from a hamper handed forth
biscuits and ham, and lemonade to drink;
and then took up three wounded men
hit by artillery rounds. Carefully

he placed them in his carriage, looking briefly
to his own now-wounded horse, and then drove
the hurt men slowly to a hospital—
one of the many barns and houses taken
by our surgeons for their desperate work.
And then this man drove back and got three more.
The sweetheart I have loved since childhood days
once told me that in a vision she'd seen
God. I doubted—little knew God's strange ways,
how hell obeys heaven. But I have seen.

And now the Ninth Corps, finally deployed,
moved forward in an undulating march
across stubble, pastures, cornfields, orchards,
stone fences, through rail fences, woods. Our boys
had waited, some of them, an hour or more
under Rebel artillery fire; now
shot and shell found them easily and tore
arms, heads, muskets, knapsacks, and ragged holes

in our lines. On the right the Ninth New York
in bright Zouave uniforms made easy marks

for the Rebels, and when they charged their line
of infantry lost half their men at once—
but rallied and continued their advance
with leveled bayonets, and with a fine
and murderous determination closed
with them and fought them hand to hand, until
the Rebels broke and ran. Charging the hill,
the Highlanders of Christ's Brigade disposed
of grayback infantry support, and forced
their batteries to skedaddle. Of course

it was too good to be true. Their center
was running through town, and our right brigades
had taken cemetery hill: the day
would at last be ours. But there were other
plans. Providence was not quite through with us.
Our left was in the air. Harland's Brigade,
the nearest to the Harper's Ferry Road,
contained the Sixteenth Connecticut,
a regiment of recruits three weeks old:
hungry, tired, knew nothing, could barely load

their new rifle-muskets—marched blindly straight
forward into forty acres of corn
that rose above their heads. Little warning
came from mounted officers, who did sight
a body of troops on their flank wearing
dark blue uniforms, and some say flying

the United States colors. They were bearing
straight in for our flank; you wouldn't ask why,
what with the usual confusion that day:
another brigade simply lost their way.

Then comes that devilish, hungry Rebel Yell.
And now from front and left their first volley—
that heavy zip, zipping—the air is filled
with bullets—the thunk and thud; your friends killed
and you can hear them—corn stalks crisply breaking—
all of it coming at you blind: officers shouting,
men shooting into the corn—curses
and screams and yells—your sweating hands shaking
as you try to load—some of the shrill sounds
are coming from yourself—you fire a round

into the air ahead of you. Their yell
is closer; now the corn is coming down
though all you can see ahead is smoke. Again
you begin to load but you've turned around
and can't think where to stand; your officers
have forgotten you—a bullet sears your
jacket and you understand they mean you—
no time to load—you don't know who ran first
but all of you are running—run together
the only way the damned shooting Rebels

aren't coming from. As all the Sixteenth runs
through the next regiment, the wracked battle
line breaks into pieces. An empty saddle—
a riderless horse, head down, is running

alongside the flooding crowd of men. Stunned
minds do not see the horse, whose rider,
their division commander, General
Isaac Rodman, lies on the field, a Rebel
sharpshooter's bullet in his chest. He dies
as his division streams away, his eyes

open toward the sky. He had seen the Rebels
coming, had been riding through that meadow
to warn his officers. First Israel
Richardson, now Rodman, two of our best.
In all, that day of battle, nine generals
will be killed, but how can the Republic
replace these two? And in the town a shell
bursts through a wall and a young crying girl
is torn by hot metal and she is killed,
and how shall our battling Republic

replace one little girl, bring back to life
one little, crying girl, bring back to life
the worlds and universes lost for this?—
reclaim the souls lost streaming from the camps
and hospitals and battlefields of this
torn and dying nation? The dim and flaring lamp
of Freedom flutters with the concussions
of our cannons, guttering in blood. Can souls
return to spent bodies? Can a nation
be born again? Lord, bless the moaning souls

of all these wandering dead. May sacrifice,
the burning bodies and the fuming minds,

be made sweet by our posterity:
so may our humble deaths raise Liberty
in the sight of the world, and raise the poor
to rule themselves with justice and honor.
We die away from the world and have nothing
here: only the future generations
can give these dry bones breath,
and give meaning to our deaths.

Army of Northern Virginia

"It is all right . . ."

A soldier-boy has few things on his mind
at times like these: to load and fire, obey
commands, look to your comrades right and left.
There's not much more can work inside a head
filled full with noise and watery with fear.
At times, it's true, you go insane in fights
and feel no fear; but most the time raw terror's
so strong and so big you can't get beside
it enough to see it. That's why you're drilled
and drilled and drilled, to move the way you're told
without you have to study on it any.
"File left!" "Guide right!" "Close up!" "Right shoulder shift!"
"Load!" "Fire!" That's the most you can do in fights.
You can't see. Anyone who tells you we
could see more than the dozen Yankees straight
ahead of us in smoke, has spent his hours
with lithographs of battles, clean and clear
as Sunday School books. It's all smoke and dust
and noise, and battle's a sheer mad riot
in the fields. I pity the new recruit.
He has no drill; the orders are a foreign

language: terror gives his orders. He's shot
or he runs, and's no use to himself or
others. Fact is, raw troops out-died veterans
at Sharpsburg two-to-one. Methuselah
be thanked, we had no recruits to speak of;
and those that were got put in regiments
well-seasoned, not like the Yanks, put them all
together in new regiments to raise
commissions for political appointees.
We didn't play at politics in war
the way they did. Of course, some say we lost
the war. But I was saying how we boys
were occupied with one or two things, plain
and simple. We didn't concern ourselves
in any way about the officers
once the ball commenced; but now I wonder
what went through a colonel's mind in battle.
He had to think for us. And I would give
all the sweethearts I ever had to know
what Marse Robert thought that day. He had to
stay calm, show calm; he had to see it all
and guess what the Yanks were fixing to do,
and know what to do with us, make not one
mistake—be not too rash but rash enough,
and dismiss fear. I wonder how churned up
the General's mind got anyhow. It came
to pass that afternoon when the Yankee
corps finally got over the southern bridge
and was lining up their three divisions
just other side of town, ready to march
in behind our right flank and cut us off

from the road to Boteler's Ford—twelve thousand
Yankees and we with about twenty-six
hundred men over there, and no fresh troops
on the left or in the broken center
to be sent. Well, General Lee was riding
behind the left—riding, finally; you know
he spent much of the campaign in a carriage
because he'd sprained his hands. That big gray, Traveler,
had spooked at something while the General stood
holding the reins, and pitched Marse Robert forward
onto his hands. But finally the Old
Man had his favorite saddled up and climbed
aboard, still half-helpless with his bandaged hands
wrapped up tight like a pair of swaddled babes.
So he rides up on this wreckage behind
the Dunker Church somewhere, a wrecked battery,
the Rockbridge Artillery from Virginia.
They have one serviceable gun; only
enough horses left alive to draw it
and a caisson. So he hails their captain.
"Limber up this gun," he orders. "General,"
a private's voice below him pleads, "are you
going to send us in again?" The Old Man
has no time for conversation with some
private addressing him—a blackened face
and disheveled hair and clothes—so he turns
the horse but then he realizes: that
voice is his son's. That thin, grimy private
is his own twenty-year-old boy, Robert.
Still disciplining him, or sorrowful,
I don't know—would give anything to know—

the General tells him, "Yes, my son, you all
must do what you can to drive those people
back." I say, what was on the General's mind
that he didn't recognize his own son?
Robert E. Lee was the grandest soldier
ever to put on a uniform: white-
bearded, tall and handsome and dignified
like the Lord God Almighty. He was even
willing to sacrifice his namesake son.
With honor, he could not allow the boy
to stay at home, or put him on his staff,
or send him up to Harvard like old Lincoln
did with his son Robert. What kind of mind
has a man like General Lee? If you want
to win a war, there must be no other
considerations. Just one thing. General
Lee and Old Jack were like that. The only
Yankee similar, I think, was that man
Grant. And Abe Lincoln of course: he was death
on our Cause, every moment, all the time,
come hell or high water. Now General Lee
had one word for it: duty. It was his
way of being a private soldier-boy:
you think of one thing—orders, to him duty—
and don't go try to think above yourself.

Well, we had two things going for us down
at our right flank. One was good old Mother Earth.
No place on that battlefield was flat
and clear and open for more than a few
hundred yards—the Cornfield was an exception—

but the southern end was like a blanket
rumpled up and shoved together. Ravines
and hollows, steeply rising little hills
and ridgelets—plunging into troughs again
like some stormy little sea. You could not
see much more than a couple hundred yards.
You could look carefully across that pretty
landscape, nary an unfriendly countenance
anywhere; and an entire division,
blue as the devil and the deep blue sea,
could be waiting stacked in three deep, directly
as you come over a rise. And that worked
for us. The second item in our favor
was A. P. Hill and his division. All
of it had stayed down in Harper's Ferry
to parole Yankees—about another
twelve thousand of them—and collect victuals
and the more durable effects of war.
The Yankees manufactured good artillery,
you must say that for them, and shells less likely
to explode right in the tubes, and clothing.
Now some might think it wrong that quite a few
of our boys, regiments of them, that marched
up from Harper's Ferry, wore brand-new dark
blue uniforms. It wasn't an intent
to deceive the poor Yanks; we flew our flags.
But war is war and not a baseball game.
If you are shoeless, wearing stinking rags,
and here are crates of government uniforms—
hell, you put them on; and you consign
your old clothes and their vermin to fondly

cherished memory. You don't arrive half
dressed at the ball. Soon as Little Powell
read his order to proceed to Sharpsburg,
he put his red shirt on so his men knew
they were hurrying to a fight, and drove
them without mercy up that river road.
Between the brigade he left to finish
nursing the Yankees, and men who dropped off
the march by hundreds, he arrived with only
three thousand men. Now correct me if I
am wrong, but according to my reckoning
that is odds of one to four against twelve
thousand Yankees. I know we Southerners
are considered barely educable,
but I believe my figure's accurate.
Now again I'd like to know what went through
General Lee's mind, looking toward his right flank
from Cemetery Hill and seeing three
divisions of those people forming up
to crush the little force was sprinkled there
to hold them back. It must have been the worst
moment of the war, or just about. General
Lee died saying, "Tell General Hill he must
come up!" So at two-thirty, A. P. Hill
rides up, saying his division's one half
hour down the road, and dashes back to hurry
them forward. I would like to know exactly
what General Lee thought and what his feelings
were as he watched the Yankees crowd his flank,
artillery behind them, the blue lines
three-quarter mile from end to end, and start

forward, sweeping down into and up over
the hollows and rises, driving straight toward
his right and rear. First thing, a Yank brigade
pushed up to our artillery beside
the cemetery. New York Yanks, they still
wore gaudy Zouave uniforms from back when
the war got started—red baggy pants, short
jackets, fezzes—easy targets but lots
of them, regiments that hadn't seen much
fighting yet. They drove our batteries off, but
then two brigades of our infantry fired
in their faces. They stood it, though. Must have
cost them half their men. Those Yank fools charged us,
bayonets and clubbed muskets: you wouldn't
believe it but they drove our boys, and then
it looked as though it was all up with us.
That near part of their line got in the streets
of Sharpsburg—the town a mess of our boys
running—stragglers breaking into houses—
splintered-up artillery carriages
dragged around by lathered, wide-eyed horses—
officers waving their swords—couriers
delayed by clots of men—black folk driving
wagons up with ammunition—barking
dogs and here and there a riderless horse
running blood. The Old Man is in the town
and sees two dust clouds Harper's Ferry way.
He comes upon an artillery captain
with a small telescope. "What troops are those?"
The captain lifts the glass, but General Lee
holds up his splinted hands. "Can't use it," he says.

The captain looks, and says, "They are flying
the United States flag." "Other column,"
the Old Man quickly asks; "what is that column
to the right?" The captain looks, and it is
a long look. Then he says, "They are flying
the Virginia and the Confederate
flags." And General Lee says—I would have bled
to hear his voice—he says, "It is all right.
It is A. P. Hill from Harper's Ferry."

Seeing the Yankee flank, Hill didn't take time
to line his division up; didn't need
to. He was striking them end-on—sent in
brigades as fast as they could leave the road,
deploy, and charge. They hit some new recruits
there on the Yankee flank and shattered them—
came at them through a field of head-high corn
and those green fellows didn't know which way
was which—drove them running and I have heard
that two of them did not stop running 'til
they reached England, for a fact. We rolled them
up as nicely as you please and sent them
skedaddling back to their artillery
along the ridge just this side of the creek.
It would have been much better to have drowned
them in the Antietam, but what was done
was good enough. They weren't about to move
that afternoon or evening—or next day,
either. We'd stopped them everywhere they tried.
The doing nearly ate up all our army
but we did it, and one thing I do not

need to know about the Old Man's thinking
is why he didn't cross the river south
the next day, used up as the Army was.
Would you have backed away in front of Yankees?

Army of the Potomac

Sorrow every way you look

The field was white with dead men's souls, their angels
ministering to them, lifting them by arms
and shoulders, pouring water from the wells
of uncreated light, bathing their faces,
releasing them from memories of harm
like cutting beaten horses from their traces.
Oh, all had turned to loveliness and peace:
the fields in flower, swallows in the trees—
so the shatter-brained survivors dreamed,
where the dead lay, and the blind wounded screamed.

The barely living slept upon their arms,
their lines three hundred yards apart that night
across the crawling fields and empty farms.
Surgeons worked by lurid, flickering light
behind the lines in sleepless, crowded barns.
And politicians put all things to right,
and preachers pondered sacred Scripture,
for some remained, and some of us were taken.

What world is turning through this burning rapture;
what kingdom coming where we dead awaken?

One day a man shall stand before our spirits
on this battlefield, where a ghostly line
watches with rifle-muskets still upright,
to thank, bless us for the unknowing sakes
of his children, and all their children's children,
and in his uncomprehending way make
our forgotten lives and deaths into praise
of our offended and forgiving God,
who gave us our incendiary days
to learn the right, and fight for what is good.

We fought over right and wrong. If slavery
isn't wrong, the President once said, then
nothing is wrong. If Lady Liberty
is good, and governments are made by men
to keep her person safe, American
Union is her only hope. It is right
to defend her. Let not her flag be furled.
The Rebels hid behind their hate. The world
of Them and Us is even simpler than
the world of black and white.

We went down South to root it out—and find
that hate cannot be rooted from the mind
by war. Yet let them hate us if they will;
the cause of Liberty is living still.
They love her less?—then we shall love her more,
'til right makes might; and, honored equally by all,

all people that on earth do dwell shall fall
before the throne of a just God, who pours
His blessing, like His lifeblood, on the free.
Surely our Creator loves humanity,
for freedom's measured by equality.

I know some will forget. One day the fight
will be too dim, its flashes thunderless
to some lost generation of the night
who, looking back, will think us innocent
and sunny, our war a brave distress,
our wives' and mothers' griefs but beads of light
that like our lives were curiously spent.
The purple larkspur in the fields in June
shall weave our garland of remembrance then.
We loved our country's children's children.

Army of Northern Virginia

Amen, I say

The tragedy of Sharpsburg sickens me—
the sheer loss from my point of view.
Future generations North and South
will call it noble sacrifice, valor,
and all the other words we've always used
for killing, being killed, rotting in the sun,
alpha and omega amen. The Cause
will set our children's children's teeth on edge
because of our peculiar institution.
Our institution was based on certain
truths you would have to call self-evident—
an arrangement benefitting both bond
and free, lifting the African above
his natural place, civilizing what
in him can reflect such benefit,
offering the waters of baptism
to the extent his childlike cup can draw,
raising his dark and fragmentary soul
out of the tribal fires of perdition.
You defend beliefs that are your birthright,
and fight for what you know. You do your best.

You protect your interests, like anybody.
Our Cause was just the constant cause that always
moves a man: defend our homes, families,
honor, and our way of life—right or wrong.
The Yankees are a mystery to me.
Sometimes I've thought them meddling fools to fight
when no one threatened them—fight for a union
we hated and despised, for the dim sake
of generations unborn, or to free
a race they detested—whatever they say
otherwise. I can't easily admire
my inferiors for being unselfish—
a gentile polyglot tribe of penny
pinchers and money-grubbers and mudsills—
for the very righteousness which they
arrogated to themselves. And I know
a lot of Yanks fought for the hell of it.
We hated them. Maybe the Yankees fought
because they're Yankees, and we Rebels fought
because we're rebels—rebels to our souls.

Emancipation is sheer ignorance.
The African is not the same as us,
the way a child is not an entire man;
and they don't feel just as we white folks do—
and if he has a soul, it's incomplete,
or likelier, it's different from a soul.
And yet the Good Lord saves them, I expect.
It's true that no white man would want to be
a slave, but we were born with certain rights
and Liberty is one of them. Black folk

are born to savagery or servitude:
they're happier the way they're meant to be.
To bind a black man to a factory
is the true and inhumane slavery;
a kindly master is a gift from God.
The Yankees and their pirate industries,
their steaming sweatshops, crowded tenements
where you can't breathe—these are what abolition
adds up to in the end. The Union's based
on hypocrisy; that is why we haunt
the battlefield, and haunt the Yankee soul.
The point is, we have tamed the African
and he belongs to us. I've thought it through:
we receive his earthly labor, and he
receives the heavenly fruits of our faith.
His is the better part of the bargain.
The abolitionists can go to hell—
and will, for causing this ungodly war.
The Yankee loves a future that does not
exist; he loves a principle, a dream.
We love what is. "The evil of the day
sufficeth; take no thought for the morrow."

But this fight puts an end to everything.
Sharpsburg has seared the heart of Secession,
emancipation staining our gallant
banner to the last sad generation.
The angry children's teeth are set on edge
because we drink the bitter swill of guilt.
The honor of the unrepentant dead
requires grief, or the liquor of cruelty.
No nobler sons of liberty ever

died for a wrong cause, a cause lost for good
to a long future haunted by the past;
or will faith in our unvanquished rage burn
in our unreconstructed children's hearts
and bleed in the bosom of Abraham
forever? Will our flaming fallen cross
rise again refined by our devotion,
purified in that Kingdom without end;
or will the faded, furled, and forlorn symbol
of our lost love be staked over our graves,
a lurid cross burning red three hundred
years in the fires of a divided nation?

I wonder if the story here starts deeper
than Rights or Union or slavery, deeper
than the North and South, and only God
knows what it is.
                    There is a Confederate
cemetery at Shepherdstown across
the river. Like all the places we lie,
it is a humble affair. Small gray stones,
a company forgotten and forlorn,
the grass mown seldom, dandelions in seed—
a Cause made kind by neglect, human pride
made dear by long-forgotten grief, the wrath
of battle settling into violets;
and now we are equal in death with all
who ever lived and died—Africans, slaves,
Yankees, colonels, presidents, and Romans.
If you'd judge the War by its cemeteries
you'd shed a tear for the South, or be chastened
by the sadness of cavaliers in rags.

With time, our stones are butternut
and gray: a hundred fifty weathering years
have withered summer's dry moss pale brown
like the spidery threads that drape our bones.
Six hundred seasons like the hand of God
have rubbed our names with rain and snow and sun,
until "Unknown" is easiest to read,
our States and ranks smoothed like old memories.
But we are here, a company in lines,
a solemn menace yet, the Stars and Bars
placed over us by someone's loving hands.
Before you send us to the elements,
dismissed from service with the stain
of slavery blackening our bony hands,
thinking you would have fought for Old Glory
and not the tattered banners of the South—
think whether you despoil God's giving earth
to get what you want, as we did; and think
whether you are too good to use each other
just as you wish; and think whether the poor
are moaning in the chains that you have made—
and all because you have the rights to do
and own just as you please: because,
standing on our graves, you are one of us.

God's tender mercy must embrace us all.
We lost the Cause and passed away, and now
the South is only us, quiet in our soil;
and to you it is a mystery why
we fought and died, and for what—what it was
to live in 1862. We're gone
and vanished deep in little graves; no flags,

no boasting, wrath, or history can bring
us back. Our voices are still, our pride spent,
our uniforms dust. The wrongs we did still
torment you but the loves we knew are all
drawn up into the heart of God, for He
receives the longing soul, and satisfies
the hungry soul with goodness unfailing.
The Cause we loved and suffered shall find mercy
in the heart of God. Amen I say, amen.

Army of the Potomac

One story

Why did they do it? Why did they stand and fight?
No other reason but contempt—the hating
kind. Lee wouldn't be run off by Yankees,
would rather leave some of his boys to rot;
for after all, the Lord was on his side
and would crown godly arms with victory.
And that is why five thousand soldiers died.
I think the Almighty loves to disguise
Himself. The poor are rich and fools are wise.
Surprise awaits all the children of pride.

The field of battle was alive with flies;
you thought the corpses moved. Horses, bloated,
burst like bags of gas. Our whole sick army
stayed at Sharpsburg and cleaned up. The old road
South never looked so good, but we waited,
for I don't know what, buried all the dead—
ours first then theirs—vomiting everything
we tried to eat, punished for victory
it seemed, yet knowing how much worse would be
leaving our dead for others to bury.

The army would have followed Little Mac
anywhere, but staying put went down hard.
The Rebs had crossed the river in one night
all whipped to hell, worn barefoot, and half-starved.
I think Mac never got his gumption back;
I think he just lost all his will to fight.
The Rebs, like us, had died in pretty rows,
sad mockeries of what had once been men;
and once you know what every soldier knows,
it takes awhile to go back in again.

Mister Lincoln came to Sharpsburg after—
the high command in not so many words,
the most solitary man in the world.
I think he was the meaning of the war.
Deep down against our will the heart obeys
the will of God, and longs in its pained way
for Him who longs for us. This old story
lies beneath it all. It is the only
story. The President was never free,
and battle's chances never were unjust.

Sometimes I think we fight because we must;
we choose to fight because we have no choice.
We fight for evil or we fight for good:
we grip the angel 'til we have been blessed.
The righteous sentence must be writ in blood;
the beauty of the lilies to be seen
must turn from flower to light and cease to be.
A deed removed to thought is understood;
the reader lifts the letters from the page.

I fought the heart's battle as did they—
you can call it love; you can call it rage—
from one, out of many, the one story:
one multitude, one heaven, and one life;
one meaning in all suffering and strife.